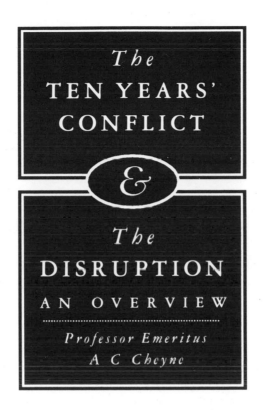

The
TEN YEARS'
CONFLICT

&

The
DISRUPTION

AN OVERVIEW

Professor Emeritus
A C Cheyne

SCOTTISH ACADEMIC PRESS
Edinburgh
1993

Published by
Scottish Academic Press Ltd.
56 Hanover Street, Edinburgh EH2 2DX

ISBN 0 7073 0742 2

The help of the Drummond Trust towards publication
is gratefully acknowledged.

Typeset by Trinity Typesetting
Printed in Great Britain by
W. M. Bett Ltd, Tillicoultry

The Ten Years' Conflict and the Disruption
An Overview

The Disruption drama of 1843 was played out against a background of astonishing change, profound and many-faceted, which left few areas of Scottish life untouched.

Socially, the country was in course of transformation by the rise of mechanised industry, the helter-skelter growth of large towns, and a population explosion which tripled the size of Glasgow between 1780 and 1815. Politically, the revolutionary Reform Act of 1832 had begun Britain's long march to universal suffrage, arousing high hopes among those who longed for a truly democratic form of government. Ecclesiastically, momentous developments were taking place both inside and outside the Church of Scotland, the state-recognised, state-supported religious 'Establishment'. Inside it, the balance of power between parties was undergoing drastic alteration. The Moderates — reasonable men, accommodating and down-to-earth, the lesser descendants of those eighteenth-century giants, William Robertson and his friends, who had made Edinburgh one of the centres of the enlightened world — no longer dominated the counsels of the General Assembly, and were fast losing both prestige and influence throughout the nation. The re-invigorated Popular party, on the other hand, strong in the enthusiasm, demonstrative piety and crusading spirit of the religious revival associated with the names of Wesley, Whitefield and Wilberforce, had already annexed the challenging title of 'Evangelical' and was now poised to take over the direction of religious affairs from its allegedly effete, reactionary and worldly-minded adversaries. Outside the Church of Scotland, the Presbyterian Dissenters (United Secession and Relief, soon to come together in the United Presbyterian Church), were growing in numbers, confidence and aggressiveness. Calling for the dis-establishment of the Auld Kirk in the interests of 'voluntary' religion, they embarrassed it not a little by drawing attention to their own superior generosity, to the ease and speed with which they could respond to the needs of an increasingly mobile population and — most important of all — to their vastly more democratic method of appointing ministers.

The conflict that ended in the Disruption began ten years earlier, when the General Assembly of 1834 passed two Acts which sought to take account of the social, political and ecclesiastical circumstances just indicated. One was the Chapels Act, the other the more famous Veto Act.

The aim of the Chapels Act was to bring about the full incorporation, within the existing ecclesiastical structure, of the new extension charges (or 'chapels') that had sprung up, especially in the Central Lowlands, as a result of the staggering increase and movement of population experienced there since the closing decades of the eighteenth century. Pushed through by the Evangelical party (from whose ranks most chapel ministers were drawn), this crucially important piece of legislation elevated the chapels to equality of status with the ancient parish churches of the land — spiritual equality, at any rate. They were assigned parish areas, clearly delimited; their government was to be by kirk sessions with full authority; their ministers became entitled to sit in all the Church courts. It is difficult to exaggerate the significance of what was a truly revolutionary measure. It consolidated the Evangelical ascendancy. It facilitated the return of Dissenting congregations to the Established Church. It gave a tremendous fillip to Church Extension, with over 200 new congregations being brought into existence by 1843. There were only two snags about it. For one thing, it increased the tension between the Church of Scotland and the Dissenters, whose clothes it might

2

be said to have stolen. For another, some critics objected that only Parliament could create new parishes. In 1834, these objections were brushed aside; but by 1843 the second in particular had become a formidable problem.

If the Chapels Act may be regarded as embodying the Church's response to social change, the Veto Act was even more obviously its answer to the transformation of the political scene. By opening the door to democratic practices in secular life, the great Reform Act highlighted their absence in the ecclesiastical realm. More and more people were being allowed to choose their political leaders: why was it only Dissenters of the Secession and Relief Churches who could choose their religious leaders? — The focus of concern here was, of course, the patronage system. Ever since the Parliament of the United Kingdom had passed the Patronage Act in 1712 (against fierce Scottish resistance), the appointment of parish ministers rested mainly in the hands of the country's landed proprietors, though the Crown had the right of presentation to some three hundred livings and quite a number of others were in the gift of urban corporations or the universities. Opposition to the system was not much in evidence during the late eighteenth and the early nineteenth century, but from about 1830 it became increasingly vocal, especially among Evangelicals. Prominent individuals like Andrew Thomson of St George's, Edinburgh called for its complete abolition; but the majority, who were no radicals, preferred with Thomas Chalmers to retain the system while introducing a popular element into it. This they sought to do by means of the Veto Act (1834), which grafted the principle of 'non-intrusion' — that is, the assertion of the inviolability of congregational freedom against all outside interference — onto the old procedure. What resulted was as follows. The patron still presented; the presbytery still examined the person named and, if he passed the test, inducted him to the pastoral

3

charge; but now an equally important role was assigned to the congregation. If they could neither initiate the process nor complete it, they *could* terminate it. According to the new Act, if a majority of the 'male heads of families' who were communicants recorded their opposition to the patron's nominee, the presbytery were obliged to reject him without further ado. In other words, a congregational 'veto' would henceforth block the 'intrusion' of an unpopular presentee. The rights of the people were at last to be given appropriate weight.

Needless to say, not everyone was happy with the Veto Act. Some (as has already been indicated) desired the total abolition of patronage. Others preferred a more gradual approach, rejecting a single piece of Assembly legislation in favour of a whole series of judicial decisions by the Church courts. All objections, however, were overborne. The Lord Chancellor, no less, expressed his approval of the proposed Act, while the Government — patron, on behalf of the Crown, in one-third of all parishes — undertook to follow the procedure which it laid down. All seemed to be set fair.

One cloud nevertheless appeared on the horizon — a cloud presaging storms of totally unexpected violence. The Moderate party in the Church, who were still a considerable body, disapproved of the Veto. Among other things, they pointed out that popularity was not always the best indicator of a minister's worth; that the new Act would almost inevitably cause friction in the parishes; that the only really significant objections to a presentee — those relating to his intellectual or moral inadequacies — could already be dealt with in the course of his 'trials for licence' by the presbytery; that it was a regrettable innovation to substitute the negative veto for the positive 'call' by the congregation (which still survived, though in a somewhat shadowy form, from earlier days); and that what the Non-intrusionists proposed came perilously near to replacing a presbyterian with a congregational polity, since presbyteries would in future be bound to accept the will of congregations on the subject of ministerial appointments. Most ominously of all, disgruntled Moderates observed that the new measure would certainty impinge upon property rights — which were a civil, not a religious matter — and so do much to alienate the most important classes in the community.

These objections, disregarded in 1834, soon returned to plague the Church. As we can see more clearly today, triumphant Evangelicalism had not faced up with sufficient realism to the awkward question: what would happen if a vetoed presentee or a thwarted patron rebelled against the operation of the Veto Act and challenged its legality in the civil courts? — The answer to that question was quickly forthcoming, and an exceedingly unpleasant answer it proved to be.

In October, 1834 the patron of the parish of Auchterarder in Perthshire, the Earl of Kinnoul, issued a presentation in favour of one Robert Young, a recently licensed probationer-minister. Young preached twice in the vacancy, but at the crucial meeting of the congregation only two parishioners signed the 'call' while a huge majority — 287 male heads of families out of 330 — registered their dissent as provided for by the Veto Act. In due course, therefore, the presbytery rejected Mr Young; and there the matter should have rested. What actually happened was very different. Encouraged by one of the most eminent lawyers of the day, John Hope, Dean of the Faculty of Advocates, Young and Kinnoul appealed to the Court of Session (Scotland's supreme civil court) against what they believed to be the illegal behaviour of the presbytery. Eventually, in March 1838, that court sustained their appeal. Its judgment was as followed: 'The said Presbytery are bound and astricted to receive and admit the pursuer as minister of the church and parish of Auchterarder, according to law.'

What could the Church do now? Meeting a few weeks later, the General Assembly made what was to prove a fateful decision. After passing an unrepentant 'resolution on spiritual independence' which harked back to similarly embattled pronouncements that had been made in the sixteenth century by Andrew Melville and in the seventeenth by the authors of the Westminster Confession of Faith, they appealed to the ultimate judicial authority in the United Kingdom, the House of Lords. A year later, they got their answer. On 4th May 1839 the two supreme law lords, Lord Brougham and Lord Cottenham, ruled that the patron's rights were absolute, that no objections by parishioners were relevant, and that in examining a presentee presbyteries should concern them-selves only with his 'life, literature and doctrine', and not with his acceptability to the congregation. In a phrase, the Veto Act was illegal, and if the Church did not accept that fact its office-bearers would meet with the full rigour of the Law — interdicts, fines, even imprisonment. As F. W. Maitland said of an equally famous judgment in 1904, 'The cold hand of the law fell on the living body of the Church with a resounding slap.'

A fortnight later, the General Assembly made a reply which combined intransigence with some indications of will-ingness to negotiate. It refused to ordain Mr Young, adducing the principle of 'non-intrusion'. But it accepted the Lords' ruling so far as the temporalities (manse, stipend etc.) of Auchterarder parish were concerned; and it appointed a special committee to treat with the Government for a resol-ution of the problems then emerging — problems which threatened both the privileges of Scotland's religious Establish-ment and a harmonious relationship between Church and State.

At this point in the narrative it may be advisable to pause for a moment and summarise the chief points at issue, not only between churchmen and their legal and political adversaries but also among churchmen themselves. The Moderate party in the Kirk, together with the civil courts, held that in an Established Church even ordination was not a purely spiritual matter: it involved civil concerns as well. They also contended that the congregational 'call' was no more than a courteous convention, and that the only essential qualifications of a minister were sound theology, adequate educational attainments and a good character — all of which were looked into by the presbytery at his 'trials'. The Evangelicals and the General Assembly, on the other hand, argued that ordination is an entirely spiritual affair, altogether separable from admission to a 'living'. Moreover, the 'call' (whose pedigree they traced back to Reformation times) was for them of fundamental importance; and they were convinced that acceptability to his people must be included among a minister's essential qualifications.

But even more profound differences than these can be discerned. One side stressed the supreme duty of civil obedience, their favourite Biblical text being Romans ch. 13 v. 1: 'The powers that be are ordained of God.' Without submission to the secular authorities, they argued, it would make no sense to talk about 'national recognition of religion', which was at the heart of Establishment. They added that only the civil courts could adjudicate impartially between Church and State. And they called for repeal of the illegal Veto Act, abandonment of emotive references to Christ's Headship over the Church (despite their current popularity in Non-Intrusionist circles), and recognition that there is no greater ecclesiastical evil than schism. The other side were concerned above all with spiritual freedom, and not infrequently quoted Acts ch. 6 v. 29: 'We ought to obey God rather than men.' They owed much to Andrew Melville's 'Two Kingdoms' theory of Church-State relations, developed during his celebrated controversy with King James VI. Church and State, they averred, have

7

each their prescribed sphere of operations, but in early nine-teenth-century Scotland the State (personified by lawyers and politicians) is encroaching — with devastating results — upon the Church's territory. In order, therefore, to maintain its God-given privileges the latter must stand firm — even, if necessary, at the cost of losing the benefits of Establishment.

Political theorists have sometimes contrasted the two views under the headings of Erastianism and Theocracy. To contemporaries in 1840 they must have looked more like the classic instance of an irresistible force meeting an immovable object.

We return now to the chronological sequence of events. Happenings similar to those that had occurred in the parish of Auchterarder took place elsewhere (in Lethendy, for example, and Culsalmond); but it was at Marnoch, in Banff-shire, that the gravity of the problems confronting the Church was most clearly revealed. The details need not be gone into, fascinating though they were. What should be noted is that this time the presbytery concerned — the presbytery of Strathbogie — had not an Evangelical but a Moderate majority. These men, soon to be famous as 'the Strathbogie Seven', reluctantly decided that in the clash between Church courts and civil courts they must, like dutiful citizens, obey the law of the land and induct a rejected presentee. For so doing they were eventually deposed from office by the General Assembly of 1841: a measure which shocked many, even within the Evan-gelical camp, and led to the rise of a 'Middle Party' who feared that the Non-Intrusion leaders, Robert Candlish and William Cunningham in particular, were steering the Church onto the rocks. Another, equally ominous, consequence of the Marnoch imbroglio was that by the spring of 1842 there were two congregations, two ministers and two kirk sessions (as well as two churches and two manses) within the parish, each claim-ing to be the true representative of the Church of Scotland!

One conceivable way out of the impasse still remained. Parliament had made the law which the civil courts were administering: could it be persuaded to alter what it had once enacted? With this hope in mind, and under the leadership of the venerable Thomas Chalmers himself, the Non-Intrusionists turned from the lawyers to the politicians and sought help at Westminster. Unfortunately for them, the situation there could hardly have been less favourable. The Whigs (in power until the late summer of 1841) happened to be largely dependent on the support of Radicals and Dissenters, neither of whom had any love for Established Churches. And as if that was not enough their leader, Lord Melbourne, evinced a deep distrust of Dr Chalmers, remarking on one occasion: 'He is a madman, and all madmen are rogues.' Little could be hoped for from that quarter. But among the Tories the prospect was equally unpromising. Still recovering from the shock of the Reform Act, they were intensely suspicious of all democratic or pseudo-democratic movements — among which Non-Intrusionism might well be included. The consequences of undermining the Patronage Act and recognising popular rights in the parishes appalled them; and their most influential figure, Sir Robert Peel (soon to become Prime Minister), had been known to speak of the Non-Intrusionists as 'the Popish Presbyterian party'. In the end, neither Whigs nor Tories were prepared to respond positively to the Church's pleas; and although several distinguished individuals — Lord Aberdeen, the Duke of Argyll, Sir George Sinclair and the future Lord Dalhousie among others — tried to find a solution, none was successful. The ultimate disappointment came as late as March 1843, when a long debate in the House of Commons ended with a decisive rejection of the call for a special Parliamentary enquiry into the state of affairs of Scotland. (Scottish Nationalists, incidentally, will not be unduly surprised to learn that a majority of MPs from North of the Border were on the losing side. Had there been a Parliament in Edinburgh the Disruption might never have occurred!)

Meanwhile, outside Parliament, events moved towards their dénouement. In May 1842 the General Assembly did what they had shrunk from doing in 1834, and expressed their support for the total abolition of Patronage. They also gave their approval to the 'Claim of Right', an assertion in elevated — and controversial — terms of the Church's spiritual independence. In November of the same year a 'Convocation' of several hundred Non-Intrusionists met in Edinburgh to stiffen resolve and finalise plans for their forthcoming rejection of Establishment as it had been known and valued in Scotland since the Revolution of 1690. In January 1843 came the Government's answer to the pleas and warnings of the previous Assembly: a firm refusal either to repeal the Patronage Act or to grant the demands of the Claim of Right. That same month, another legal decision made things even worse. Giving judgment in the Stewarton case, the Court of Session repeated what they had done a few years previously with the Veto, and declared the Chapels Act to be illegal. Their ruling in this instance had peculiarly baneful implications for the Non-Intrusion cause, since it meant that chapel-of-ease ministers were no longer entitled to sit in the courts of the Church, and consequently that the Evangelicals would almost certainly lose the dominance over the General Assembly which they had enjoyed since 1834. An Assembly vote in favour of Disruption (a formal severing of the traditional alliance between Church and State) was suddenly rendered much less likely. As they considered the various choices now open to them, the Non-Intrusionist leaders therefore came to the conclusion that what today's military would call a pre-emptive strike was their best hope of snatching victory out of almost certain defeat. The time for debate was in any case past. The time for solemn affirmation and sacrificial action had come —

10

affirmation and action which would not only forestall, but also cast into the shade, anything which their adversaries might subsequently decide or do. The dramatic events of 18th May 1843 were the result.

When the Assembly met that afternoon in St Andrew's Church the retiring Moderator, Professor David Welsh (a leading Non-Intrusionist), broke with routine. Instead of making up the roll of members and installing his successor, he read out a lengthy Protest against the conditions being imposed on the Church by the State — conditions which made it impossible for him and his associates to accept the privileges of Establishment any longer. He then left the chair and the building, followed by some two hundred ministers and elders who shared his views. Through an excited crowd, and joined by many sympathisers, they processed to the Tanfield Hall in Canonmills, where they constituted themselves 'The Church of Scotland — *Free*', and signed a Deed of Demission renouncing the many benefits of Establishment. The long-heralded Disruption had at last taken place, and the Free Church — the most vital and thrusting of nineteenth-century Scotland's religious bodies — was launched upon its remarkable career.

There can be little doubt that what had just taken place was the most important event in Scotland's religious history since the establishment of Presbyterianism in 1690. For the ministers who 'went out' (some 450, eventually, out of a total of around 1200), it involved very considerable sacrifices: the renunciation of churches, manses, glebes, stipends — and social standing. For the members who accompanied them (between one-third and one-half of the whole), it meant facing up to financial demands greater than any the Church had previously made upon them. For the entire nation, it meant some erosion of its distinctive identity, and an accelerated movement into an ordering of things where the State rather than the Church presided over such essentials of community life as poor relief and education. For true religion, it brought both loss and gain. Loss, because of the slow extinction of the ancient ideal of the Church as the focus of unity and service in every parish, and because of the bitter animosities that divided Auld Kirk and Free Kirk over several decades. Gain, because of the flood of energy, enthusiasm and generosity which was released in the youthful Free Church, leading (at home) to the building of hundreds of new churches, manses and schools, as well as theological colleges of international repute, and (abroad) to the development of missionary endeavour on a scale and of a quality hardly surpassed by any other communion in the English-speaking world.

The historiography of the Disruption is a study in itself, and can hardly be entered into here. But it may be worth noting that most scholars of the present generation are much less inclined than their predecessors were to concentrate on the religious aspects of the story. Today's favoured approach is through sociology; and if its exponents have not said the last word on the subject they must certainly be credited with contributing much that is stimulating and persuasive. Foremost among them is Dr Allan MacLaren, author of *Religion and Social Class: the Disruption Years in Aberdeen* (1974). Ignoring theological questions altogether, MacLaren concentrates on the social circumstances which made possible the emergence of the Free Church in the provincial capital of the North-East and largely explain its subsequent development. In particular, he highlights the conflicting interests of two groups within the city: the old dynasties of top families (lawyers and merchants for the most part, quite often with landed connections), and the emergent, entrepreneurial middle class (men of obscure origins but increasing wealth, socially and geographically mobile, who 'having been denied accommodation by their social superiors increasingly sought confrontation with them'). It was this latter group who, according to MacLaren, found their way into the Non-Intrusionist camp, and after the Disruption 'were to direct the new Church along its initial dynamic course, shape its organisation, make it a success as a denomination, and having achieved their own ambition and proved their ability, leave it with unsolved problems such as its role as a twin to the Established Church'.

To balance MacLaren's work with a contribution of a much more theological flavour, the late Professor Ian Henderson's *Power without Glory: A Study in Ecumenical Politics* (1967) is well worth examining, and equally provocative. Discussing the run-up to the events of 1843, Henderson points to what he considers a fatal error on the part of early nineteenth-century Evangelicalism. It had, he suggests, 'a perfectly legitimate and indeed laudable central political object, the abolition of the 1712 breach of the Act of Union' (the Patronage Act). But in order to gain its ends the Evangelical party 'transposed its activities into a theocentric key. By taking to itself the great name of the Evangel, and not some colourless designation like that of the Moderates, its rival party, it successfully conveyed the idea that to oppose it was to oppose the Gospel'. He therefore concludes: 'The will of God was thus once again in the saddle of the Church of Scotland. And as in the sixteen-forties the result was disaster', since 'any ecclesiastical party which identifies its policy with the will of God has got a hold of the right formula for breaking the Church of Scotland. For it is a formula which precludes discussion, and makes possible lovelessness and even prayer against one's brother in Christ'.

Incidentally, Henderson's remarks point us to a notable — and perhaps somewhat overlooked — aspect of the Disruption period: that is, the general unwillingness of the participants to conciliate or mediate or concede anything. One thinks not only of leading Non-Intrusionists like Robert Candlish, William Cunningham and Hugh Miller, but also (on the other side) of John Hope, Lord Brougham and the Tory Home Secretary, Sir James Graham. Their bellicosity seems to mirror the confrontational attitudes of an entire society. It was an age of crusades and campaigns — not only the Voluntary Controversy and the Ten Years' Conflict, but Chartism and Owenite Radicalism and the Anti-Corn Law League as well: an age in which claims tended to be pitched at their highest, and the language of denunciation stretched to its limits. That Scotland was not unique even in the realm of ecclesiastical warfare is demonstrated by the early history of the Oxford Movement, whose leaders used language not unlike that which came from the lips of Chalmers and his colleagues — as when, in his famous sermon of July 1833 on 'National Apostasy', John Keble exclaimed: 'How many [Church members] continue their communion with the Church *established* (hitherto the pride and comfort of their lives) without any taint of those Erastian principles on which she is now to be governed? What answer can we make henceforth to the partisans of the Bishop of Rome when they taunt us with being a mere Parliamentary Church?' If the Ten Years' Conflict split the Church of Scotland, the Tractarians' war with liberal thought and State interference tore Oxford apart, sorely divided families like the Wilberforces, and if it did not split the Church of England in the eighteen-forties has come near to doing so in the nineteen-nineties. The whole sad tale of early-Victorian bellicosity does not excuse the virulence of pamphlets, sermons and Assembly speeches which afflicted (and excited) the Scottish public between 1834 and 1843; but it may at least persuade us to view them with a little more understanding.

Before concluding, there is one question to which we must attempt an answer: was Non-Intrusion a worthwhile cause, and can the Disruption be justified?

Almost simultaneously with the walk-out of 1843, Sir William Hamilton, the distinguished Edinburgh philosopher, addressed the would-be secessionists in a pamphlet entitled, 'Be not Schismatics, be not Martyrs by Mistake'. His argument was that Non-Intrusion had never been a Calvinist or Presbyterian principle, and that religious believers should be grateful to the civil magistrate, whose worldly wisdom was capable of checking the aberrations of over-enthusiastic divines. More than a century later, another eminent Edinburgh academic, Professor Gordon Donaldson of the chair of Scottish History, bade fair to flutter the ecclesiastical dovecotes in like manner. The essay on 'Church and Community' in his *Scottish Church History* (1985) is an attack on the Melvillian 'Two Kingdoms' theory which underlay the Non-Intrusionists' programme. In characteristically forthright language, Donaldson remarks that 'The frequent assertion that "Christ is the sole King and Head of the Church" settles nothing. The Kingship of Christ over His Church is acknowledged by all. What is at issue is not the Kingship of Christ but the agencies on earth through which the heavenly Kingship is exercised.' And he goes on to contend that 'preoccupation with the Kingship of Christ over His Church may be actually dangerous', as it is 'apt to lead to a view of the State as purely secular': 'The One-Kingdom theory, on the other hand, sanctifies the State as well as the Church, seeing them both as alike subject to the Kingdom of Christ.' Professor Donaldson (we may presume) would not have 'gone out' in 1843; and when we recall how speedily the Disruption led to secularising measures like the withdrawal of Poor Law administration from Church control in 1845, and of education from Church control in 1872, we cannot but acknowledge that he has a point.

But there is much — very much — to be said on the other side. It is an impressive fact that two of the most learned and penetrating political theorists of the twentieth century, the left-wing Socialist, Professor Harold Laski, and the Anglo-Catholic divine, Father Noel Figgis, should agree in commending the Disruption as a prime example of the defence of ecclesiastical freedom against the encroachments of State power. For Figgis's closely-argued thesis, reference must simply be made to his *Churches in the Modern State* (2nd edition, 1914). Laski, however, is irresistibly quotable. His *Studies in the Problem of Sovereignty* (1st edition, 1917) contains the assertion that 'The Presbyterians of 1843 were fighting the notion of a unitary State', and goes on to observe that 'If the State, theoretically, was in the event victorious, practically it suffered a moral defeat. And it may be suggested that its virtual admission in 1874 [when Patronage was abolished] that the Church was right is sufficient evidence that its earlier resistance to her claims had been mistaken.' And he concludes: 'A State that demands the admission that its conscience is supreme goes beyond the due bounds of righteous claim. It will attain a theoretic unity only by the expulsion of those who doubt its rectitude. It seems hardly worthwhile to discuss so inadequate an outlook.'

Britain's most eminent living Church historian, Sir Owen Chadwick, comes down — in the end — on the same side. Admittedly, he deplores the fact that Chalmers and his companions could not wait. 'Legal systems', he writes, 'are always more flexible than they look; even lawyers have hearts beneath their waistcoats of chain-mail; quietness and patience and persuasion are no less Christian virtues than is the heroic sacrifice of stipends on high principle.' Yet his final words on the Ten Years' Conflict are much more positive. 'Nevertheless', he concludes, 'the headship of Christ is that without which churches may as well be swept aside into heaps of rubble or converted into gymnasia. In all the span of Christian history one can find no clearer demonstration of the sacred appeal to that headship, in the realm of ecclesiastical polity,

16

than in the events of 1842-43 and the leadership of [Thomas Chalmers].' ('Chalmers and the State', in A. C. Cheyne [ed.], *The Practical and the Pious* [1985].)

A final observation. When the broken parts of Scottish Presbyterianism came together again in the Union of 1929, they did so on the basis of an agreed statement — the so-called Declaratory Articles — which discussed, along with various other topics of fundamental importance, the relationship between Church and State. It included the following carefully chosen words: 'This Church, as part of the Universal Church wherein the Lord Jesus Christ has appointed a government in the hands of Church office-bearers, receives from Him, its Divine King and Head, and from Him alone, the right and power subject to no civil authority to legislate, and to adjudicate finally, in all matters of doctrine, worship, government and discipline in the Church, including the right to determine all questions concerning membership and office in the Church, the constitution and membership of its Courts, and the mode of election of its office-bearers, and to define the boundaries of the spheres of labour of its ministers and other office-bearers. Recognition by civil authority of the separate and independent government and jurisdiction of this Church in matters spiritual, in whatever manner such recognition be expressed, does not in any way affect the character of this government and jurisdiction as derived from the Divine King and Head of the Church alone, or give to the civil authority any right of interference with the proceedings or judgments of the Church within the sphere of its spiritual government and jurisdiction.' That momentous statement, to which the Parliament of the United Kingdom gave its carefully-considered assent, was only made possible (it may with confidence be asserted) by the trials and tribulations, the struggles and the sacrifices, of the men and women of the Disruption.

NOTE ON FURTHER READING

A valuable but simple introduction is G. D. Henderson, *Heritage: A Study of the Disruption* (1943), which was published as part of the centenary commemoration.

More advanced, and wider in scope, is *Scotland in the Age of the Disruption* (1993), a collection of essays edited by S. J. Brown and M. Fry for the 150th anniversary. Its notes point the way to further study.